First SCIENCE

ELECTRICITY

By
Steffi Cavell-Clarke

ST. ALBERT PUBLIC LIBRARY
5 ST. ANNE STREET
ST. ALBERT, ALBERTA T8N 3Z9

KidHaven
PUBLISHING

Published in 2018 by
KidHaven Publishing, an Imprint of Greenhaven Publishing, LLC
353 3rd Avenue
Suite 255
New York, NY 10010

© 2018 Booklife Publishing
This edition is published by arrangement with Booklife Publishing.

All rights reserved. No part of this book may be reproduced in any form without permission in writing from the publisher, except by a reviewer.

Designer: Danielle Rippengill
Editor: Charlie Ogden

Cataloging-in-Publication Data

Names: Cavell-Clarke, Steffi.
Title: Electricity / Steffi Cavell-Clarke.
Description: New York : KidHaven Publishing, 2018. | Series: First science | Includes index.
Identifiers: ISBN 9781534523869 (pbk.) | 9781534523845 (library bound) | ISBN 9781534524774 (6 pack) | ISBN 9781534523852 (ebook)
Subjects: LCSH: Electricity–Juvenile literature.
Classification: LCC QC527.2 C38 2018 | DDC 537–dc23

Printed in the United States of America

CPSIA compliance information: Batch #CW18KL: For further information contact Greenhaven Publishing LLC, New York, New York at 1-844-317-7404.

Please visit our website, www.greenhavenpublishing.com. For a free color catalog of all our high-quality books, call toll free 1-844-317-7404 or fax 1-844-317-7405.

PHOTO CREDITS

Abbreviations: l-left, r-right, b-bottom, t-top, c-center, m-middle.

Front cover – Luis Molinero. 2 – Sergey Novikov. 4 – Brian A Jackson. 5– Tom Wang. 6 – Lucas Sevilla Garcia. 7 – Rawpixel.com. 8l – ProstoSvet. 8r – Roman Yastrebinsky. 9 – Atsushi Hirao. 10 – Neil Mitchell. 11 – yelantsevv. 12 – SkyLynx. 13 – OKAWA PHOTO. 14 – AlinaMD. 15 – Naruden Boonareesirichai. 16 – Rawpixel.com. 17 – haryigit. 18 – sirastock/iStock/Thinkstock. 19l – Lolostock. 19m – Gelpi. 19r – janthonymartinez/iStock/Thinkstock. 20 – espies. 21 – Dmytro Vietrov. 23 – Sergey Novikov. Images are courtesy of Shutterstock.com, with thanks to Getty Images, Thinkstock Photo, and iStockphoto.

CONTENTS

PAGE 4 What Is Science?
PAGE 6 What Is Electricity?
PAGE 8 Using Electricity
PAGE 10 Where Does Electricity Come From?
PAGE 12 Electricity from the Wind
PAGE 14 Electricity from the Sun
PAGE 16 Making a Circuit
PAGE 18 Staying Safe
PAGE 20 Saving Electricity
PAGE 22 Let's Experiment!
PAGE 24 Glossary and Index

Words that look like **this** can be found in the glossary on page 24.

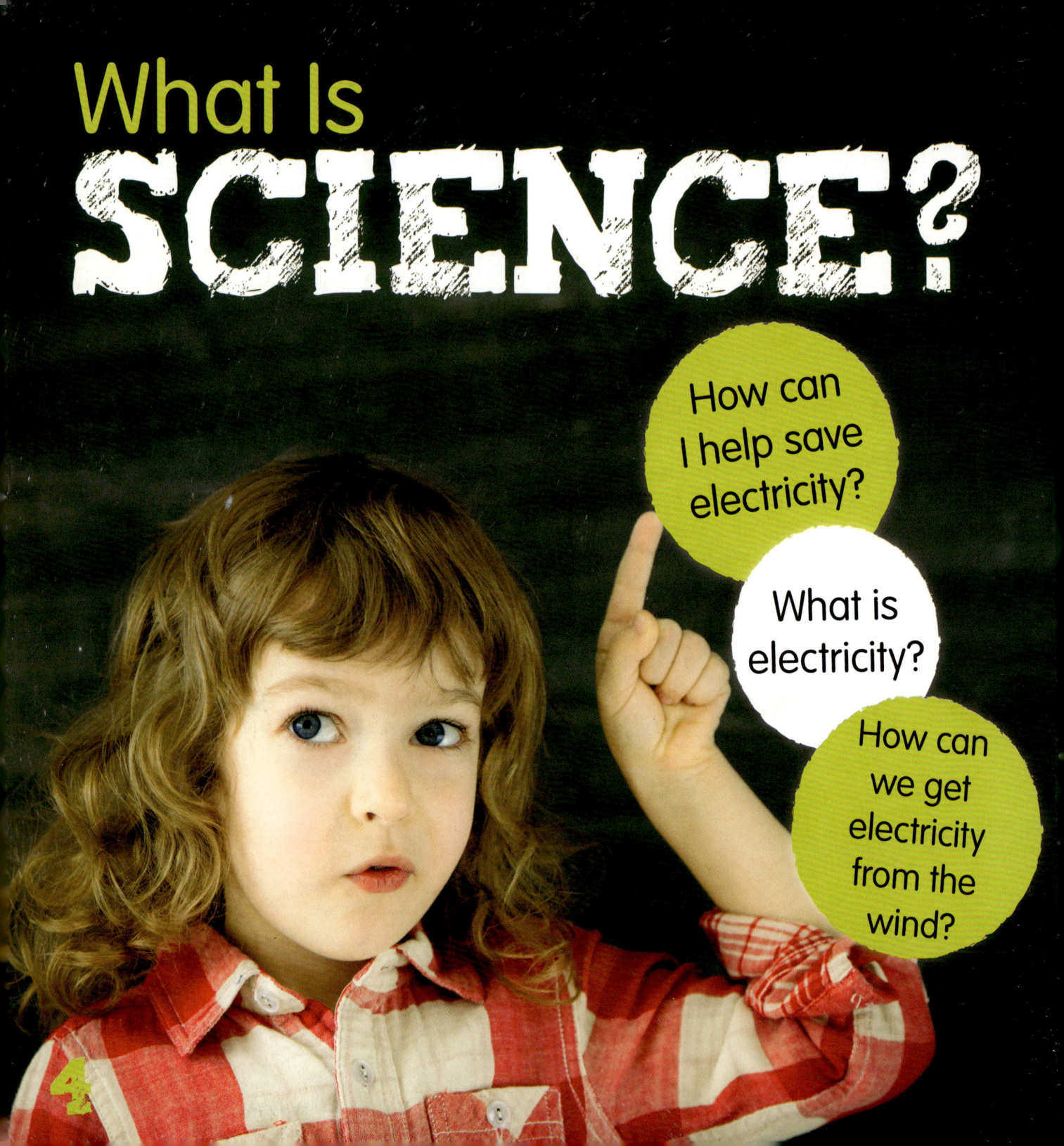

What Is SCIENCE?

How can I help save electricity?

What is electricity?

How can we get electricity from the wind?

Science can answer many difficult questions we may have and help us understand the world around us.

What Is ELECTRICITY?

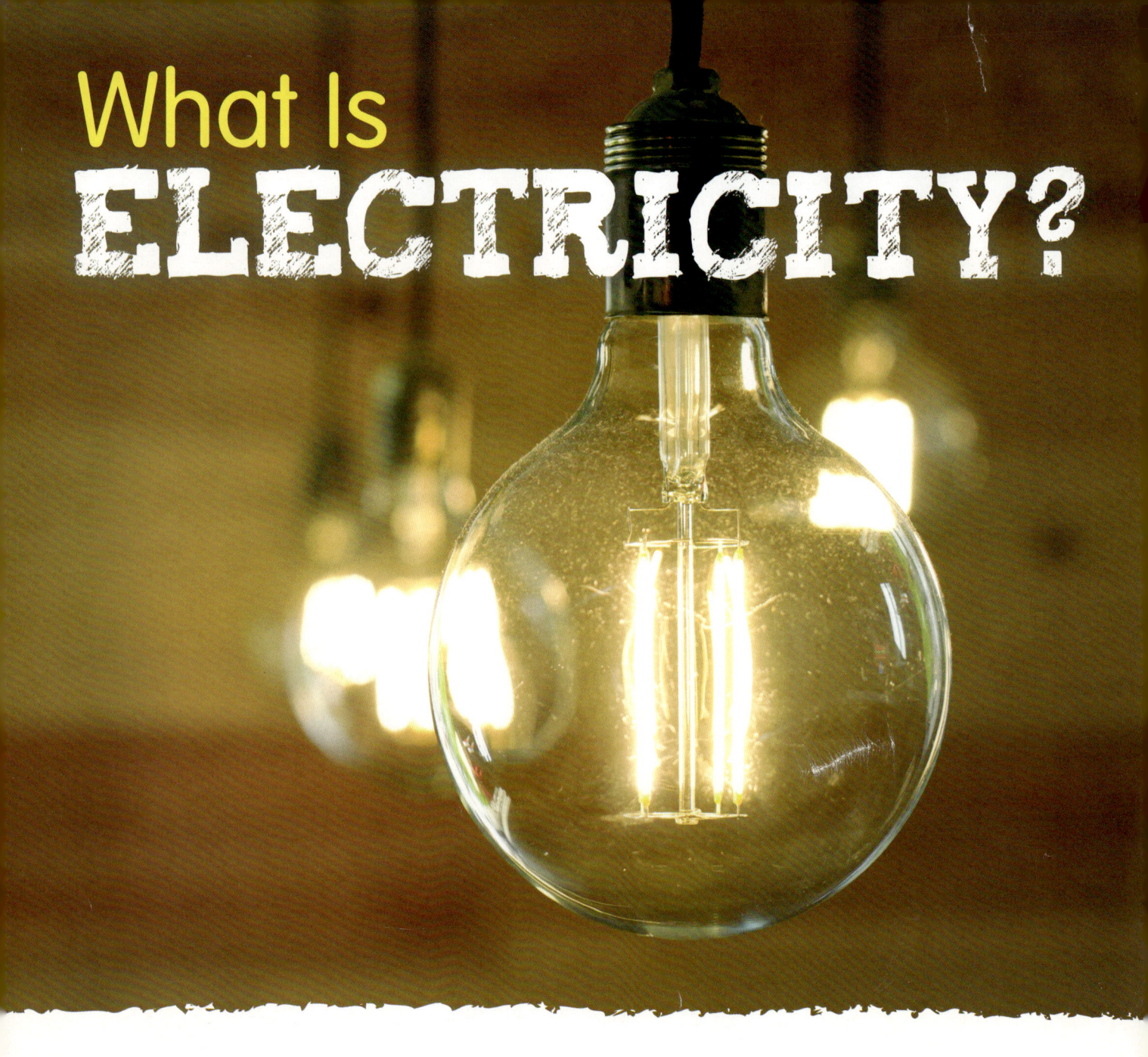

Electricity is a type of **energy** that gives things power. Most people use electricity every day.

A lot of things need electricity to work. The radio, the television, and the telephone all need electricity to work. These things are called electrical **appliances**.

Using ELECTRICITY

Lamps use electricity to make light.

Radios use electricity to make sound.

Electrical appliances need to be plugged into **sockets** and switched on before the electricity can power them.

Electrical appliances have a switch that turns the flow of electricity on and off. When the switch is on, electricity flows through the socket.

Never play with sockets. They can be very dangerous!

sockets

9

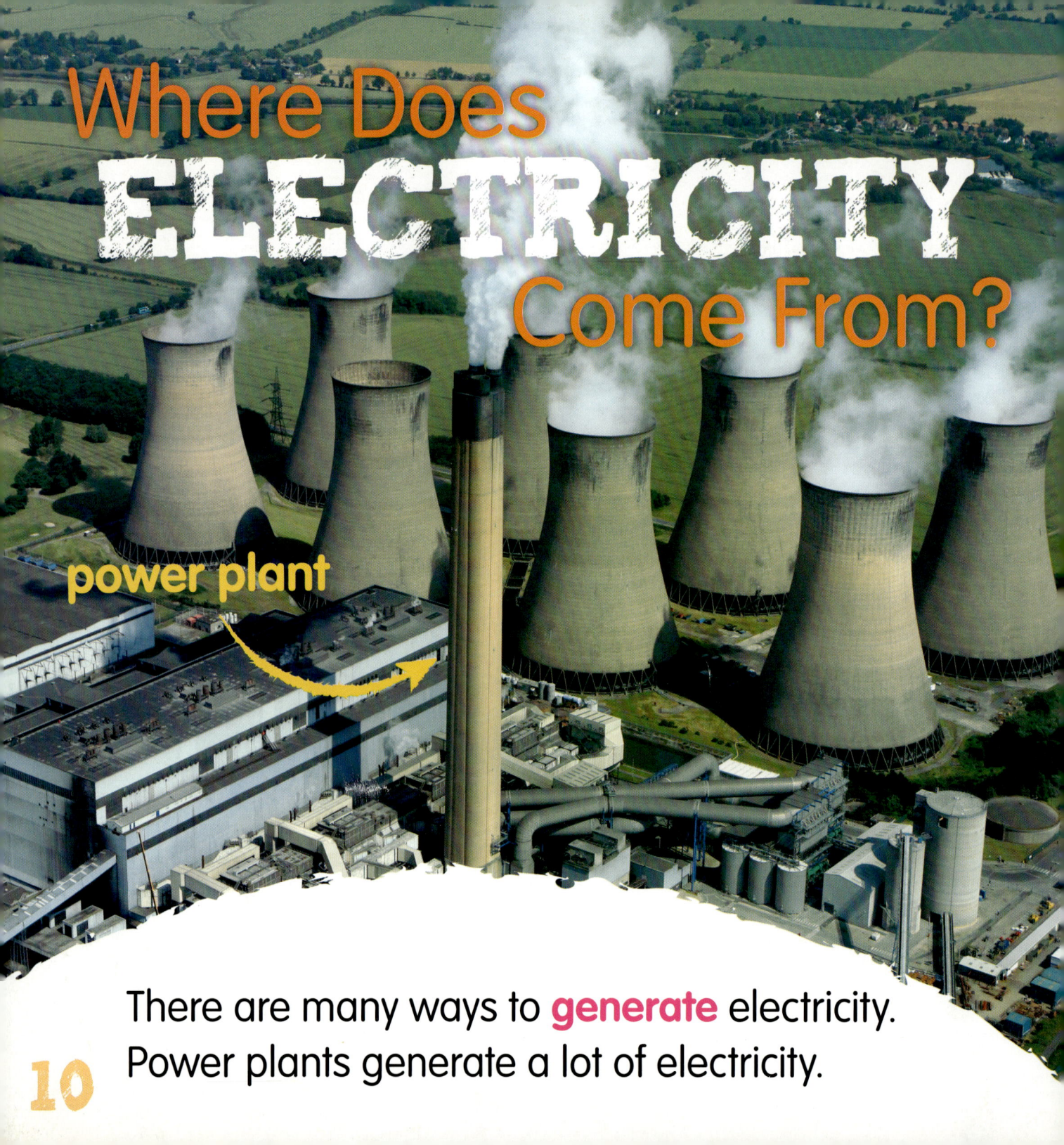

Where Does ELECTRICITY Come From?

power plant

There are many ways to **generate** electricity. Power plants generate a lot of electricity.

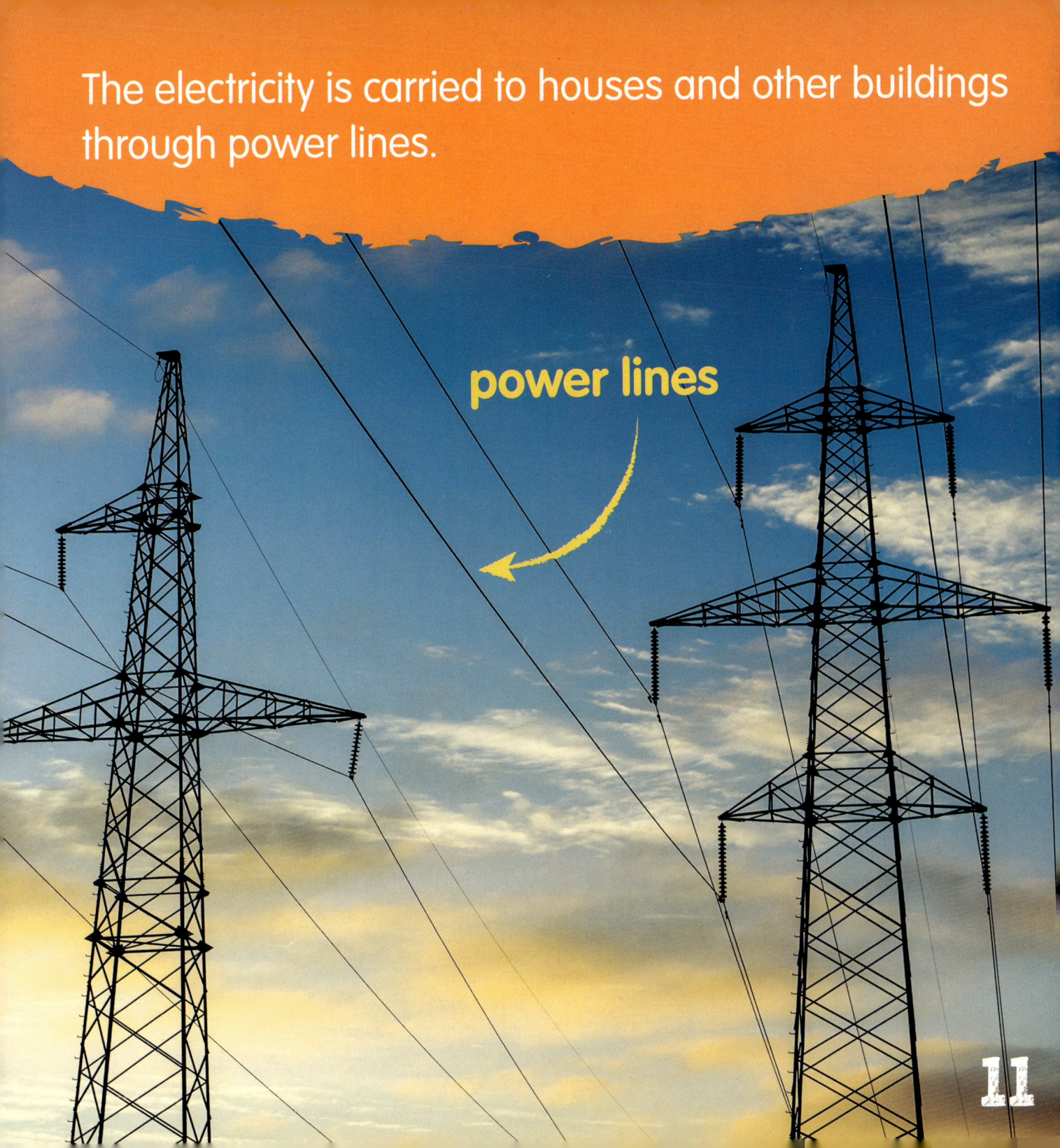

The electricity is carried to houses and other buildings through power lines.

power lines

11

Electricity from
THE WIND

wind turbine

blades

Wind turbines generate electricity using the wind. The wind turns the blades on the wind turbines.

As the blades turn, the wind turbines generate electricity.

Electricity from THE SUN

Sunlight can be used to generate electricity. This is called solar power.

14

The sun shines its light on a solar panel. The solar panel uses the energy to generate electricity.

solar panels

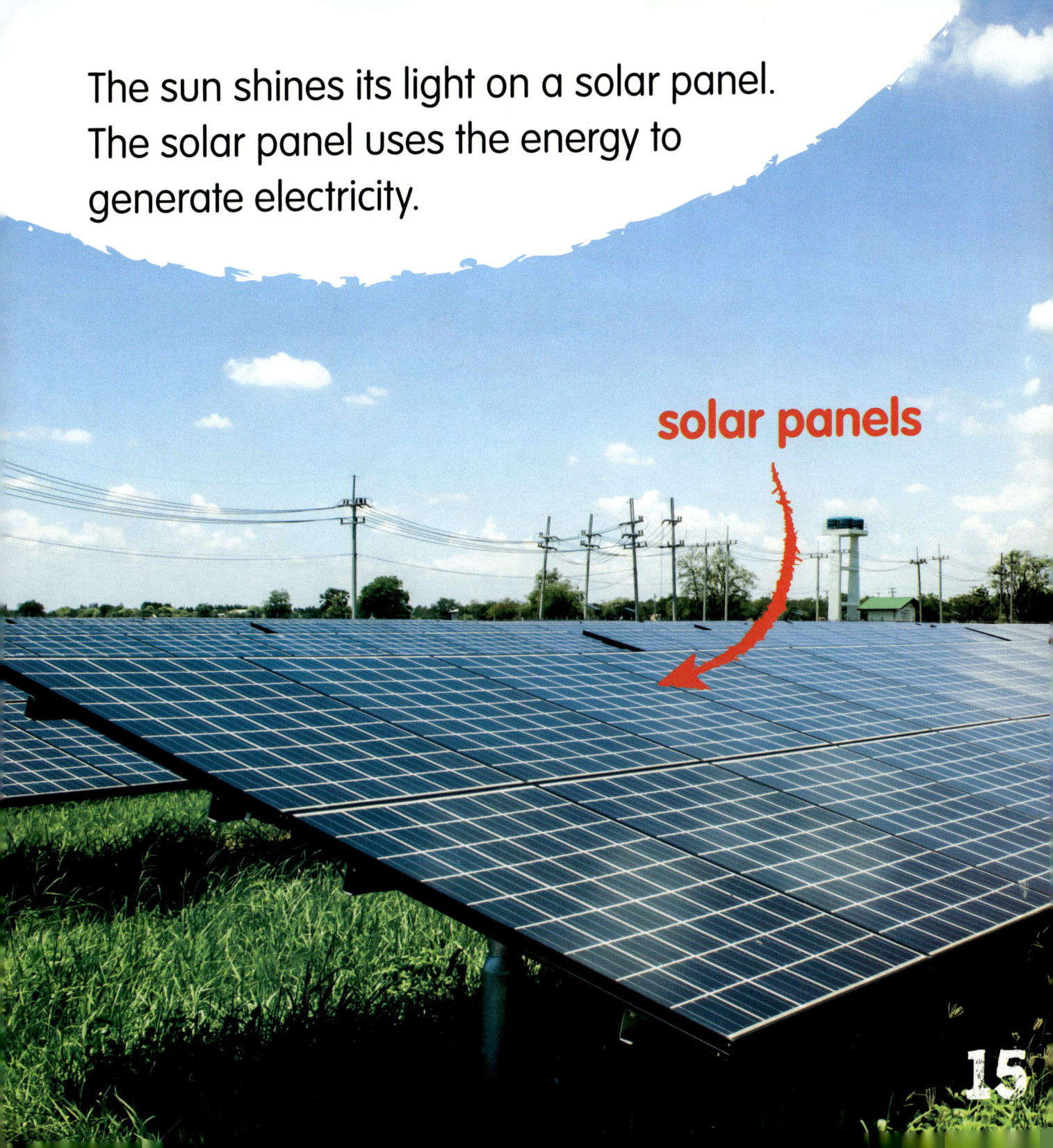

Making a CIRCUIT

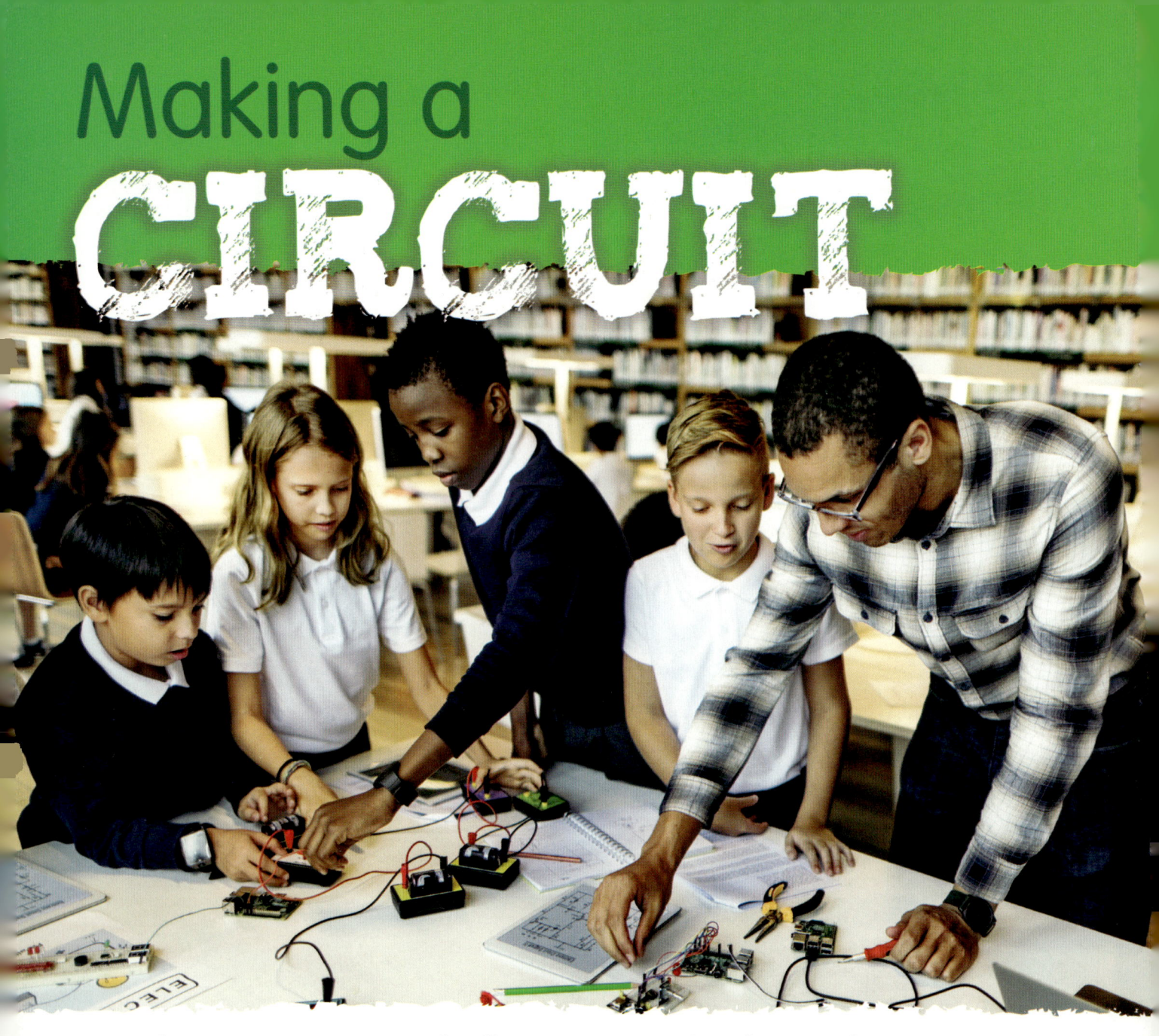

Electricity can only flow around a loop that is complete. This loop is called a circuit.

An electrical circuit is made up of parts called **components**. The components are joined together by wires. The electricity flows through the wires and to the components.

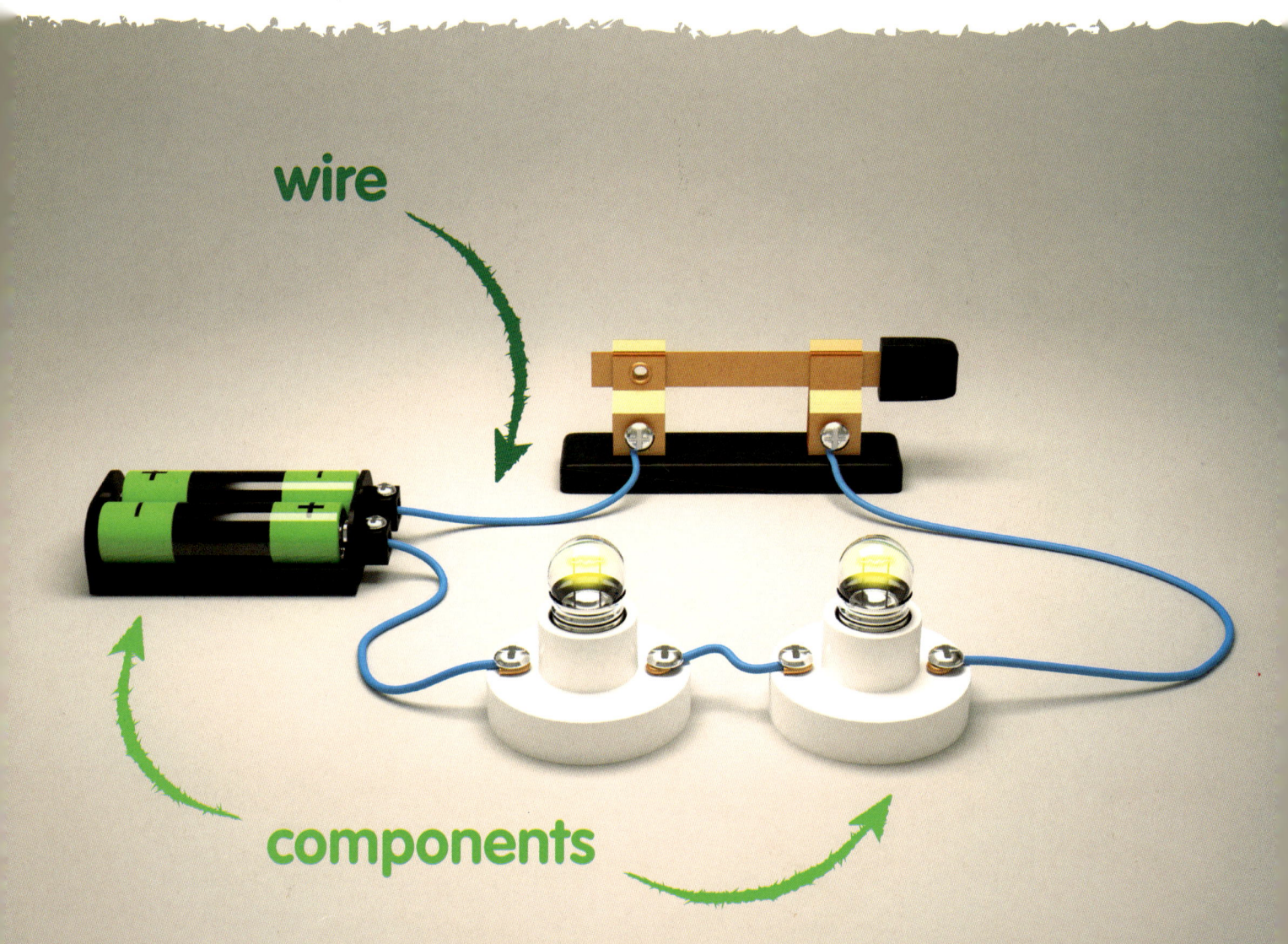

wire

components

Staying SAFE

Electricity can be very dangerous. It is important to always be careful when using electricity and electrical appliances.

Stay safe, and remember these top safety tips:
- Never put your fingers in sockets.
- Keep metal items out of toasters.
- Never use any electrical items around water.
- Never pull a plug out of a socket by its cord.
- Do not plug many appliances into one socket.

Saving ELECTRICITY

It is very important to save electricity. Generating electricity can be hard on the environment and expensive, so it is important not to waste any.

Every time you turn off a light or switch off an appliance, you are saving electricity. Remember to always switch electrical appliances off when you are not using them.

Let's EXPERIMENT!

Do you know how to make a circuit? Let's find out!

YOU WILL NEED:
alligator clips
plastic-coated wires
a light bulb
a light bulb holder
batteries
a battery holder

STEP 1
Before you can light up the light bulb, you need to make a circuit. First, screw the light bulb into the light bulb holder, and make sure the batteries are safely in the battery holder.

STEP 2
Connect one end of each wire to the battery holder using the alligator clips.

STEP 3
To complete the circuit, use the alligator clips to connect the opposite ends of the wires to the light bulb holder.

TOP TIP: Ask an adult to help you!

RESULTS:
Your light bulb will light up! This is because electricity can travel from the battery, along the wires, through the light bulb, and back to the battery again.

GLOSSARY

appliances things that can be used for a special task
components things that do a job in a circuit
energy power used for an activity
generate to produce or create electricity
sockets electrical devices that hold a plug

INDEX

batteries 22–23
circuits 16–17, 22–23
light 8, 14–15, 21–23
plugs 8, 19
power plants 10

safety 18–19
sockets 8–9, 19
solar power 14–15
wind turbines 12–13
wires 17, 22–23

ST. ALBERT PUBLIC LIBRARY
5 ST. ANNE STREET
ST. ALBERT, ALBERTA T8N 3Z9